THE AWESOME NIGHT SKY

First published in 2018 by Wayland
Copyright © Wayland 2018

Wayland
Carmelite House
50 Victoria Embankment
London EC4Y 0DZ

Managing editor: Victoria Brooker
Creative design: Paul Cherrill

ISBN: 978 1 5263 0594 7

Printed in China

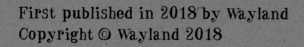

FSC
MIX
Paper from
responsible sources
FSC® C104740
www.fsc.org

Wayland is a division of
Hachette Children's Books,
an Hachette UK company.

www.hachette.co.uk

THE AWESOME NIGHT SKY

Written by
Kay Barnham

Illustrated by
Maddie Frost

WAYLAND

Did you know that there are millions and millions
of stars in the universe? During the daytime,
the sky is too bright for us to see stars.
But in the night sky, they twinkle and shine.

How many stars can you see?

Our Sun is a star.
It is much closer to us
than other stars, which
is why it looks so big.
(The Sun is so bright, you
must never stare at it!)

The Sun is *very* important. It warms
our planet and gives us light.
It makes plants grow. Without the Sun,
there would be no life on Earth.

Earth is just
one of the planets
that travel around
the Sun. The planets
nearest the Sun
are very hot.

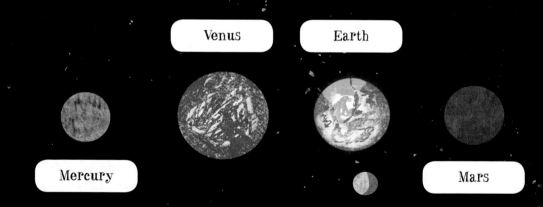

The planets closest to Earth shine
in the night sky. Look out for Mercury,
Venus, Mars, Jupiter and Saturn.

The planets furthest away are very cold. On our planet, the temperature is just right.

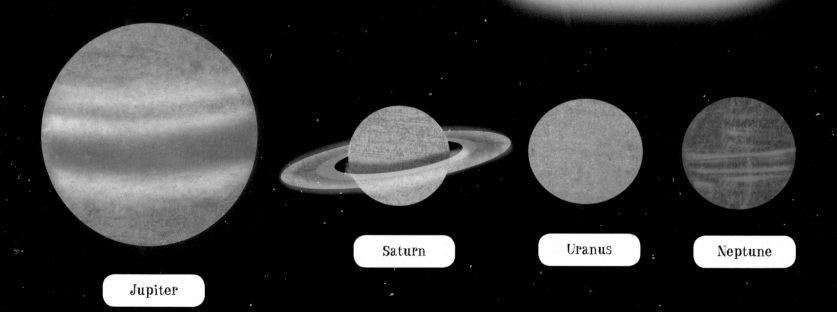

Jupiter

Saturn

Uranus

Neptune

The Moon is a ball
of rock that travels
around our planet.
It is the biggest object
in the night sky.

We can see the Moon because
it reflects sunlight. As the Moon goes
around Earth, we can see different
amounts of the sunlit part of the
Moon. This is why it looks as if
the Moon changes shape.

A galaxy is a group
of many, many stars.
There are billions
of galaxies in the
universe.

Our Sun is part of a galaxy called
the Milky Way. We can sometimes see
the middle of the Milky Way.
It looks like a misty smudge
across the night sky.

A constellation is a group of stars that
makes a pattern in the night sky. Long ago, people
thought that if they joined the stars together,
the shapes looked like people, animals or objects.

Orion is a famous constellation that can be seen from all round the world. Orion was a hunter in an old Greek story.

Did you know that a shooting star
is not a star at all? It is a piece
of dust or rock called a meteor.
This burns brightly as it falls
through the atmosphere – the layer
of gases around Earth.

When many meteors fall
at once, they are called
a meteor shower.

Asteroids are large pieces of rock
that are too small to be planets.
But like planets, they travel around the Sun.

A comet is a huge lump
of ice and dust that follows
a huge oval path around the Sun.
When it is near the Sun,
it has a bright tail.

Astronomers study
the objects in space.
They look at the planets
that travel around
the Sun. They look at
distant galaxies.
They try to find out
how stars begin and end.

We do not yet know
everything about the universe.
But astronomers are helping
us to find out more.

The universe is huge.
Things we see in the night sky
can be very, very far away.
Astronomers use telescopes
to see objects in space.

The Hubble Space Telescope is in space!
It helps us to see things much more
clearly than telescopes on Earth.

Another way of finding out about space
is to go there. Spacecraft carry astronauts into space.
Powerful rockets push them high above our planet.
Then they travel around Earth.

Last century, astronauts landed on the Moon.
So instead of seeing the Moon in the
night sky, they saw Earth!

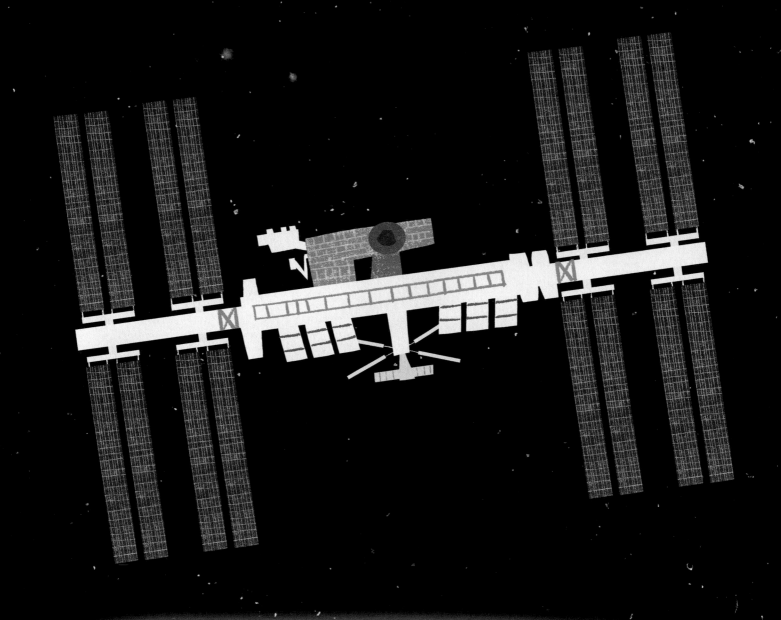

Sometimes, you will see a bright light
moving slowly across the night sky.
This is the International Space Station.
It is a place where astronauts live and work.

The space station travels around our planet more than 15 times a day!

In the future, humans hope to travel a very long way. But first they need to find out more about the universe. Space probes are spacecraft that go on long, long journeys into space.

They send back information to Earth about what they find.

Rovers are robot vehicles
that explore the planet Mars.
It is the nearest planet to Earth
– one day, humans hope to live there!

THINGS TO DO

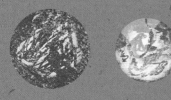 

1. Make your own night-sky picture. Paint a big sheet of paper a very dark colour and once it has dried, decorate it with stars, a moon, planets, rockets and anything else you can think of!

2. On the next starry night, look carefully at the moon. The next day, make your own fabulous moon picture. It could be a painting or a collage or a pencil sketch.

3. Make a word cloud about the night sky! Start with 'NIGHT SKY, then add any other words this makes you think of. Write them all down using different coloured pens. Start like this...

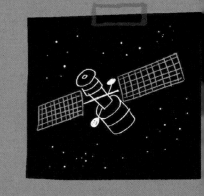

STARS MOON NIGHT SKY

NOTES FOR PARENTS AND TEACHERS

This series aims to encourage children to look at and wonder about different aspects of the world in which they live. Here are more specific ideas for getting more out of this book:

1. Use a planisphere or night-sky app to find stars, planets and constellations in the night sky with children.

2. Make a papier-mâché solar system for the classroom, using balloons for planets.

3. Ask children to build a space probe from junk. It will need a really futuristic name!

5. Put on a play entitled 'Mission to Mars'. Ask children to imagine what their trip will be like? What will they find when they land on Mars? How will they survive?

6. Look at the night sky and join the dots to make your very own constellation. Decide what or who it looks like and give it a starry name.

NIGHT SKY BOOKS TO SHARE

Astronauts (First Explorers)
by Campbell Books and illustrated by Christiane Engel
(Campbell Books, 2017)

i-SPY in the Night Sky
by Storm Dunlop
(Collins Michelin i-SPY Guides, 2016)

Little Kids First Big Book of Space
by Catherine D Hughes and illustrated by David Aguilar
(National Geographic Kids, 2012)

Our Solar System series
by Mary-Jane Wilkins
(Wayland, 2017)

The Darkest Dark
by Chris Hadfield
and illustrated by the Fan Brothers
(Macmillan, 2017)

READ ALL THE BOOKS IN THIS SERIES:

A Stroll Through The Seasons
ISBN: 978 0 7502 9959 6

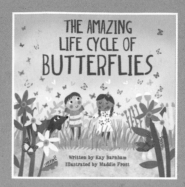

The Amazing Life Cycle Of Butterflies
ISBN: 978 0 7502 9955 8

A Wonderful World Of Weather
ISBN: 978 1 5263 0540 4

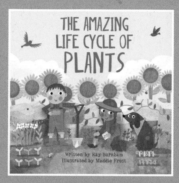

The Amazing Life Cycle Of Plants
ISBN: 978 0 7502 9957 2

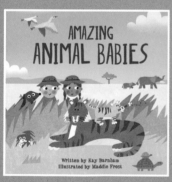

Amazing Animal Babies
ISBN: 978 1 5263 0592 3

The Awesome Night Sky
ISBN: 978 1 5263 0594 7

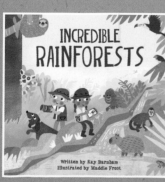

Incredible Rainforests
ISBN: 978 1 5263 0590 9

The Great Big Water Cycle Adventure
ISBN: 978 0 7502 9951 0